First Grade Fun Fitness & Learning

52 Large-Group Activities and
49 Hands-On Practice Pages
to Energize and Teach Young Students

by
Sabena C. Maiden

Key Education
an imprint of Carson-Dellosa Publishing LLC
Greensboro, North Carolina
www.keyeducationpublishing.com

CONGRATULATIONS ON YOUR PURCHASE OF A KEY EDUCATION PRODUCT!

The editors at Key Education are former teachers who bring experience, enthusiasm, and quality to each and every product. Thousands of teachers have looked to the staff at Key Education for new and innovative resources to make their work more enjoyable and rewarding. We are committed to developing educational materials that will assist teachers in building a strong and developmentally appropriate curriculum for young children.

PLAN FOR GREAT TEACHING EXPERIENCES WHEN YOU USE EDUCATIONAL MATERIALS FROM KEY EDUCATION

About the Author

Sabena Maiden is a former preschool and middle school teacher who taught for more than 10 years before making the move to publishing. She was hired by a leading educational publisher as a copywriter in advertising and later transferred to product development to work as a book editor. Since starting a family, she is now a freelance writer and editor. Having helped produce dozens of books, her work primarily includes educational, Christian, ESL, and literacy publications.

Dedication

To Laura Young and Cindy Douglas who get their first graders moving and learning every day. We thank you. And, always to my very own little learners and husband. I love you so!   S. M.

Credits

Content Editor and Layout Design: Debra Olson Pressnall
Copy Editor: Karen Seberg
Inside Illustrations: Vanessa Countryman
Cover Design: Annette Hollister-Papp
Cover Photographs: © Digital Vision and © ShutterStock

Key Education
An imprint of Carson-Dellosa Publishing LLC
PO Box 35665
Greensboro, NC 27425 USA
www.keyeducationpublishing.com

Fragrance Activity—See page 28.
Caution: Before beginning this activity, ask families' permission and inquire about students' scent sensitivities and/or allergies.

Balloon Activity—See page 34.
Caution: Before beginning any balloon activity, ask families about possible latex allergies. Also, remember that uninflated or popped balloons may present a choking hazard.

Printed in the USA • All rights reserved.

ISBN 978-1-602681-15-6
01-335118091

Table of Contents

Introduction 4

Fun with Fitness
Animal Walks 5
Fitness at School 6
Fitness at Home 7

Fun with Language Arts
Word Lists: Word Families 8–9
Word Lists: Compound Words 9

Phonological Awareness/Phonemic Awareness
Syllable Strut 10
Spread the Sounds 11
Closing Consonant Digraphs 12
Hoppin' to Rhyme 13

Phonics
A Classy Blend 14
A Vowel Howl 15
The Long and Short of It 16

Print Concepts—Sight Words, Alphabetical Order, Capitalization & Punctuation
Frequency Frenzy 17
Letter Tag 18
Word Lineup in ABC Order 19
Up & Down Letters 20
Ending Exercises 21

Grammar—Parts of Speech
Plural Practice 22
Moving with Verb Endings 23
Sentence Scramble 24

Vocabulary—Compound Words, Contractions, Antonyms & Adjectives
Acting Out 25
Shortened Words 26
Active Antonyms 27
Thinking of Sense-ational Words 28
Fancy Word Face-Off 29

Fun with Math
Numbers & Operations
Jump-a-Thon 30
In Perfect Order 31
A Greater Game 32
All Mixed Up! 33

Balloon Bop or Pass! 34
Quick Counting 35
Estimation Station 36
2, 4, 6, 8, Skip Counting Sure Is Great! 37
Add-a-Rep 38
Equation Invasion 39
Sneaky Subtraction 40
Stand & Sit Subtraction 41
Fraction Action 42
Coin Counting 43

Algebraic Thinking—Patterns, Sorting & Classifying
Predictable Patterns 44
Detecting the Rule 45
Sorting Stations 46

Data Collecting & Graphing
Fun with Fitness & Math 47

Geometry—Recognizing Shapes
The Shape of Things 48
Shape Patterns 48–49

Measurement—Length & Telling Time
Going to Long Lengths 50
Hands Above the Rest 51

Fun with Science
Life Science & Earth Science
Blooming Science 52
Animal Antics 53
Animal Patterns 53–54
Stone Sort 55
Weather Workout 56

Fun with Geography & Social Studies
Go Get It Globe! 57
Continents Patterns 57–58
Movin' with Maps 59
The Rules Rule! 60
Patriotic Parade 61

Standards Correlations
Correlations to NASPE Standards 62
Correlations to NCTE/IRA Standards 62
Correlations to NCTM Standards 63–64
Correlations to National Science Standards 64
Correlations to NCSS Standards 64

Introduction

As a primary-grade teacher, you know the best way to learn is by doing. Well, *First Grade Fun, Fitness & Learning* is all about "doing learning." This resource of ideas is meant to get students physically active while engaging their thinking processes. Most first graders are very excited—and so ready—to learn. How about harnessing that good energy and making it work to enliven your lessons! There are plenty of moments for children to sit at their desks and focus quietly on what you are teaching. And, that is important. However, many lessons that target vital life skills and academic concepts can also get kids moving while learning and thoroughly enjoying the experiences!

First Grade Fun, Fitness & Learning is designed to build children's knowledge through very engaging lessons. Students will be bursting with excitement as they participate in 52 large group activities, using locomotor or nonlocomotor movements while applying their thinking skills and responding individually or as a whole group to answer the questions. These energizing lessons are followed by reinforcing activities—half-page exercises for individualized skill practice. *To conserve paper and save time, you might wish to prepare a master copy by including a second version of the activity on the same sheet before duplicating it.*

Improving overall fitness and motor skill development while fostering academic skills is possible. So, get your students moving; get them learning with activities from this book!

How to Use the Book

Note that many of the movement activities can be completed in a classroom; however, some of the games will require an open space in which to move or run around. If a large, safe, indoor space is not available, complete those activities outside on a sunny day. Suggestions for locomotor movements are provided; it is best to vary the movements to keep children engaged in the activity. Locomotor movements include:

- gallop
- hop on one foot
- jump
- leap
- march (high stepping)
- skip
- slide feet to move sideways
- stomp
- tiptoe
- waddle on heels

Finally, in addition to providing gross motor activities, help your students improve their flexibility by taking "stretch breaks" at certain times during the day. Here are a few ideas for you:

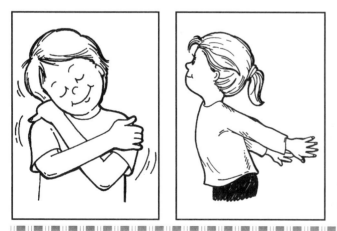

Animal Walks

Create lively relays with animal walks. Divide the class into several teams and have the players stand behind a starting line. Set out a few cones to mark the path (straight, zigzag, or weave around a line of cones) for each team. Then, explain to the players how they will move through the course. Be sure to keep the activity fun by changing the animal walk for each round of play: Game 1—lumber along like a bear, Game 2—leap like a deer, Game 3—walk like a crab, and so on. You may also wish to include other challenges at certain points along the path, such as

walking along a taped line on tiptoes or heels or balancing a beanbag on the shoulder or top of head while walking. Add your own creative ideas to keep the animal-walk relays fresh and engaging!

Alternatively, enlarge and copy the pictures below on card stock. Laminate the sheet for durability and then cut out the cards. Create fitness challenge stations throughout a large open space by setting out the equipment and the directions with pictures for performing certain movements.

Horse Gallop

Penguin Waddle

Deer Leaps

Walrus Walk

Crab Walk

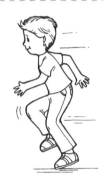

Lame Dog Limp

Kangaroo Jumps

Bear Walk

Elephant Walk

Fitness at School

Set up a fun indoor or outdoor fitness challenge for students to complete. Locate a clear, open space and mark off two large square areas, one for each team, on the floor or ground. Label each corner of the squares with a letter (A–D) and have Corner A be the starting point for each course. At each of the other corners, place an empty ice cream bucket in the center of a large activity ring. Gather 12 beanbags.

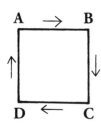

Form three groups of students, making sure that each team has an odd number of players. Designate one of the groups as line judges and arm them with pencils and papers for tallying points. Then, assign each judge one of the corners (B–D) of a course. A seventh judge will total the game points.

Have each team choose a course and line up at Corner A. Explain to the teams that each player will move (run, skip, gallop, etc.) through the course two times: once as a runner who tosses a beanbag into each container and once as a runner who retrieves the beanbags. When a player tosses a beanbag into the container without stepping inside the ring or stopping to aim, that player earns a point for the team. The first team to finish the game also earns an additional five points. Be sure to have students play again, letting the line judges become runners to complete the physical challenge against another team.

Name _____

To the Teacher: Enlarge the chart before making copies.

Be Cool and Move!

My favorite game or exercise for getting fit was . . .	Monday
Tuesday	Wednesday
Thursday	Friday

Fitness at Home

Discuss with children that they are growing bigger and stronger every day. Talk about how the decisions they make daily for eating good foods, sleeping enough hours, and exercising their bodies can help them stay healthy. Explain to children that they are going to do a fun fitness test. Demonstrate each exercise and then let each child complete it. Mark the children's efforts on a class chart that you have prepared. Make photocopies of the chart below and send home a copy of the form with each child. Take a few minutes each day to exercise with the children and encourage them to exercise at home as well to help them prepare for the fitness test. At the end of the four weeks, recheck the children by having them perform the exercises. Record that information on your class chart. Collect the "Getting Fit at Home" charts and then meet with each child individually to note any improvements that have been made.

Child's Name

Getting Fit at Home

Dear Parents and Guardians,

During the next four weeks we are working on improving our fitness. Please help your child become stronger by exercising. Once a week for four weeks, please check your child's fitness. Also, during this time, please encourage your child to be active to improve flexibility, muscle strength, and endurance. Return the completed chart on _____. Thank you for your assistance.

	Week 1	Week 2	Week 3	Week 4
Running in place (How many minutes?)				
Rope jumping (How many jumps?)				
Straddle toe touches (How many?)				
Sit-ups with knees bent (How many?)				

Word Lists

Word Families

-ab	sag	-ang	rash	-ed	ten	vet	-ig	-in
cab	tag	bang	sash	bed	then	wet	big	bin
crab	wag	clang	smash	fed		yet	dig	chin
dab		fang	trash	led	**-end**		fig	fin
drab	**-am**	gang		red	bend	**-ib**	pig	grin
grab	clam	hang	**-ast**	shed	blend	bib	rig	pin
jab	ham	rang	blast	sled	end	crib	twig	shin
lab	jam	sang	cast		lend	fib	wig	skin
nab	slam		fast	**-eg**	mend	rib		spin
tab	swam	**-ank**	last	beg	send		**-ill**	thin
	yam	bank	mast	leg	spend	**-ick**	bill	tin
-ack		blank	past	peg		brick	chill	twin
back	**-amp**	clank			**-ent**	chick	dill	win
black	camp	crank	**-at**	**-elf**	bent	flick	drill	
crack	champ	drank	bat	elf	cent	kick	fill	**-ing**
jack	clamp	flank	cat	self	dent	lick	gill	bring
lack	damp	plank	chat	shelf	lent	pick	grill	cling
pack	lamp	rank	fat		rent	quick	hill	fling
rack	stamp	sank	flat	**-ell**	sent	sick	mill	king
sack		tank	hat	bell	spent	slick	pill	ring
shack	**-an**	thank	mat	dwell	tent	stick	skill	sing
smack	bran	yank	pat	fell	went	thick	spill	sling
snack	can		rat	sell		trick	still	sting
tack	fan	**-ap**	sat	shell	**-ess**	wick	will	swing
track	man	cap	spat	smell	bless			thing
	pan	clap	that	spell	chess	**-id**	**-im**	wing
-ad	plan	flap		swell	dress	bid	brim	wing
bad	ran	map	**-ath**	tell	less	did	dim	zing
dad	tan	nap	bath	well	mess	hid	him	
glad	than	rap	math	yell	press	lid	rim	**-ink**
had	van	sap	path			rid	slim	blink
mad		slap		**-em**	**-et**	skid	swim	brink
sad	**-and**	snap	**-eck**	stem	bet	slid	trim	clink
	band		check	them	get			drink
-ag	bland	**-ash**	deck		jet	**-ift**	**-imp**	link
bag	hand	cash	fleck	**-en**	let	drift	blimp	pink
brag	land	clash	neck	den	met	gift	chimp	rink
flag	sand	dash	peck	hen	net	lift	limp	shrink
lag	stand	flash	speck	men	pet	shift	skimp	sink
rag		mash		pen	set	swift		stink
								wink

-ip	mist	-ock	fog	shop	-uck	-ull	run	-ush
dip	twist	block	frog	stop	buck	dull	sun	brush
hip		clock	hog	top	cluck	gull		crush
lip	-it	dock	jog		duck	hull	-ung	flush
rip	bit	flock	log	-ot	luck	lull	clung	hush
sip	fit	lock		blot	puck	skull	flung	rush
tip	hit	mock	-omp	cot	stuck		hung	slush
yip	kit	rock	chomp	dot	truck	-um	rung	
zip	lit	shock	stomp	got	tuck	gum	stung	-ust
	pit	smock		hot		hum	swung	crust
-int	sit	sock	-ond	not	-uff	sum		dust
hint	spit		blond	pot	bluff		-unk	gust
lint		-od	bond	slot	cuff	-ump	bunk	just
mint	-ix	cod	fond	spot	gruff	bump	chunk	must
print	fix	nod	pond	trot	huff	clump	junk	trust
	mix	pod				dump	skunk	
-ish	six	rod	-op	-ox	-ug	grump	stunk	-ut
dish			chop	box	bug	jump	sunk	but
fish	-ob	-oft	clop	fox	dug	lump		cut
swish	blob	loft	drop		hug	plump	-up	gut
wish	cob	soft	flop	-ub	jug	slump	cup	hut
	glob		hop	cub	mug		pup	nut
-ist	rob	-og	mop	rub	rug	-un	sup	rut
fist	snob	clog	plop	sub	tug	bun		
list	sob	dog	prop	tub		fun		

Compound Words

backfire	birdhouse	doorbell	handbag	houseboat	seasick
backhand	buttercup	doorstep	handball	housecoat	starfish
backrest	butterfly	doorstop	handbook	housetop	starlight
backstop	campfire	firefly	homemade	housework	sunlight
bathroom	catfish	firelight	homeroom	moonlight	sunset
bathtub	cookbook	fireman	homesick	raincoat	topcoat
bedbug	cookhouse	fireplace	homework	rainfall	treetop
bedroom	cupcake	football	horseback	rowboat	tugboat
bedtime	daylight	footrest	horsefly	sailboat	
birdbath	daytime	footstep	horseman	sailfish	
birdcage	doghouse	goldfish	horseshoe	seashell	

Syllable Strut

Get everyone ready for this fun listen-and-move activity. Prepare the area by hanging large number cards (1–4) from the ceiling or tape them to the floor. Divide the class into three teams. Explain to students that they must determine how many syllables a word contains and then move by doing exaggerated lunges to stand near the corresponding numeral. Give each team a word to figure out and watch the action. Repeat as time allows.

Alternatively, let pairs of students scatter under/near the various numerals and have them say a word based on their chosen number. If the corresponding word is correct, the team walks with lunges to the side of the room. Continue the game until the area has been cleared; then have each team choose a new number for another round of play.

Word List

blue	bumpy	butterfly
bowl	carpet	cabinet
chair	cookie	constantly
clouds	happy	elephant
crab	monkey	frequently
door	oven	grasshopper
fish	pencil	happiness
flag	puppy	library
glass	rainbow	microwave
plate	river	
red	soapy	alligator
smart	speedy	automobile
steps	table	caterpillar
whale	tiger	exclamation

Name

Say the name of each picture. Count the syllables and write the number in the box.

Try This! Can you think of a word that has three syllables? Four syllables? Tell a friend.

Spread the Sounds

Engage your kinesthetic learners with this game! Divide the class into teams and have students stand in a line, one behind the other. Give a playground ball to the first player in each line. Start the game by saying a certain word (from the word list on page 8 or 9), such as *man*. Students will separate the word into its individual phonemes. The first player passes the ball over her head and says the first sound in the word, /m/. The next player passes the ball through his legs and says the next sound he hears, /a/. The third player in line passes the ball back overhead and says the ending sound of the word, /n/. When the word is sounded out, the next player in line holds the ball and announces the word again to signal a brief stop in the game so that you can call out a new word. The player with the ball then starts the next word, like *flame*, by saying its first sound, /f/, and passing the ball back through her legs to the next student. Have the players continue the alternating ball pass. When the last student in line is given the ball, he runs to the front of the line to keep the ball in play. If students falter or incorrectly speak the word sound, pause briefly and assist them. Continue the game as time and interest allow.

Alternatively, use increasingly longer words as students improve at isolating phonemes in words.

Name _____

Colorful Sounds

Say the name of each picture. Tell how many sounds are in the word by coloring the correct number of boxes.

Closing Consonant Digraphs

Have students stand in a large circle. Explain that they will be listening carefully for ending consonant sounds (digraphs). Demonstrate which exercise will be completed for each ending sound. Also, explain to students that after you say a word, they must echo it and perform the related exercise. Continue this until students recognize the correct ending digraphs.

Exercises

-ch	forward punch
-ck	jumping jack
-sh	waist twist
-th	reach jump (raise hands over the head and jump)

Word List

-ch	search	kick	-sh	sash	depth
beach	watch*	knock	brush*	smash	fourth
bench	wrench*	lick	bush	splash	growth
branch		lock*	cash	squash	health
bunch	-ck	neck	crash	squish	length
catch	back	pack	dash	stash	math
crunch	black	quack	dish*	swish	month
ditch	block	rock	fish*	trash*	mouth
each	brick	sack	fresh		path
fetch	check	sock*	gash	-th	smith
inch	chick	stack	hush	bath*	south
latch	clock*	stick	mash	beneath	tooth*
march	crack	track	push	both	wealth
peach	deck	trick	rash	breath	with
perch	duck	truck*	rush	cloth	wreath

These words are pictured on the activity sheet below.

Name _____

Sounds to Splash!

 Say the name of each picture on a towel. Circle the two pictures that have the same ending sound.

More Sounds to Splash! Work with a friend. Tell another word that ends with the same sound as the pictures you have circled on the towel. Then, color its star.

Hoppin' to Rhyme

Keep your class "hopping" with excitement over rhyming words! First, line up students in three rows and have the child in front of each line face you. Say a word (choosing one from the list on this page or on page 8 or 9), such as *glad*. Direct the first child in each line to tell a rhyming word (for example, *dad–had–sad*). After saying an answer, each student hops quickly to the back of the line. Then, the next three students say rhyming words for a new word.

Reading Word Chunks: Select a few phonograms and write them on sections of sentence strips. Play the game again, but this time display the word chunks and have students tell you the rhyming words. This game will prepare students for the activity below.

Word Families*

_ad	lap	_et	_ig	kin	drop	jug
bad	slap	bet	big	pin	flop	mug
dad	snap	get	dig	shin	hop	plug
had	tap	jet	fig	skin	mop	rug
glad	trap	let	pig	spin	plop	slug
mad		met	rig	tin	shop	smug
sad	_en	net	wig	thin	stop	snug
	den	pet		twin		tug
_ap	hen	set	_in	win	_ug	
cap	men	vet	bin		bug	
chap	pen	wet	chin	_op	chug	
clap	ten	yet	fin	bop	dug	
flap	then		grin	chop	hug	

These phonograms are featured on the activity sheet below.

Name _____

Leapin' for Rhyming Words

- Work with a friend.
- Do the following steps.
- Write three rhyming words for each word chunk on a sheet of paper.
- Color each lily pad when done.

1. Stand up and stretch.
2. __ ad
3. __ et
4. __ ig
5. Wave your arms 5 times.
6. __ op
7. __ ug
8. __ in
9. Leap like a frog. Do 5 leaps.
10. __ ap
11. __ en
12. Do 5 leaps. You are done!

A Classy Blend

Gear up for this "classy" activity by preparing game cards. Write the letters of 12 common blends individually on pieces of card stock, four cards for each blend. (See the Word List). Divide the class into four teams. Give each team a set of cards. Call out words and have the players from the teams take turns giant stepping to the front of the room with the corresponding card.

Alternatively, set up work stations around the room with paper and pencils. At the top of each paper, write a common consonant blend (*bl-, br-, cl-, cr-, dr-, fl-, fr-, gl-, gr-, pl-, pr-, sl-, sm-, sn-, sp-, st-, sw-, tr-, tw-*). Pair students and challenge them to list as many words starting with the assigned blend as possible in two minutes. Then, have students take a 20-second refresher break by running in place before moving to the next station and adding words to a new list. Continue to rotate students around the room.

Word List

bl-	cl-	dr-	fr-	pl-	sl-
black	clap	dragon	freckle	place	slap
blanket	class	dream	freeze	plane	sled
blend	clean	drink	fright	plant	sleep
blew	climb	drive	frog	plate	sleeve
block	clock	drop	front	player	slice
blouse	closet	drum	frown	pliers	slippers

br-	cr-	fl-	gl-	pr-	sm-
bracelet	crab	flag	glad	present	smack
braid	cracker	flame	glance	press	smash
brain	crate	flap	glass	pretty	smell
branch	cricket	flat	glitter	price	smock
bridge	critter	float	globe	princess	smog
brush	cry	flower	glue	prize	smudge

Name _____

Add a Blend

Say the name of each picture. Write the missing letters.

_____ ove   _____ um   _____ incess   _____ obe

_____ ame   _____ ee   _____ og   _____ ocks

Hunt for Words! Think of or find more words that begin with the same sounds. Cut out the boxes and glue them onto a sheet of paper. Write each new word under the correct picture.

A Vowel Howl

Students will have a "howling" good time with this phonics game. First, write each featured phonogram in the list on three sheets of card stock to make the game cards. (If interested, see pages 8 and 9 for more phonograms with vowel digraphs.) Then, divide the class into three teams and give each one a set of phonogram cards. Have each team member be responsible for one or two cards. Explain to students that you will call out words which they will match by showing the corresponding phonograms. The first team to hold up a correct card gets to stand and give a rousing three-second "vowel howl." Continue the game with other words.

Alternatively, add phonograms with vowel diphthongs to the card set. Have students write each word on the board, using their game cards to help spell it.

Word List

-ail	-ay	-eak	-eam	-eet	-oad
hail	clay	beak	beam	beet	load
mail	may	weak	dream	feet	road
nail	play	creak	scream	meet	toad
sail	spray	sneak	stream	street	
tail	say	speak	team	sweet	

-ain	-each	-eal	-ee	-eep	-oat
brain	beach	deal	bee	bee	boat
chain	peach	meal	knee	knee	coat
drain	reach	seal	see	see	float
pain	teach	squeal	free	free	goat
rain	preach	steal	tree	tree	

Name _____

Rhyming with Word Chunks

Say the name of each picture. Write the missing letters.

_____ ail

_____ _____

_____ eal

_____ _____

_____ eep

_____ _____

_____ oat

_____ _____

Hunt for Words! Think of or find one or more words that are in each of these word families. Write them on the back of this paper.

The Long and Short of It

Here's another thinking-and-moving game for students to play! First, write various words with short or long vowels sounds individually on sheets of card stock. (See pages 8 and 9 for word list.) Then, have students stand in a circle. Explain that they must listen carefully to words you will say to distinguish each word's vowel sound. When you say and show students a word that has a short vowel sound, they must crouch down close to the floor to become short in height. But, when you say and show a word that has a long vowel sound, students must extend their arms out and stand on one foot to "fly" like planes. Play the game as time and interest allow.

Name

Read and cut out the words. Glue each word on the tub in the correct space.

Short Vowel Sound   Long Vowel Sound

bite	bus
on	came
ate	hen
take	cut
at	like
bit	cute

Frequency Frenzy

Learning to read sight words can be a lot of fun! Prepare for this reading frenzy by writing sight words on index cards (see word list). Make 15–20 word cards for each station, one station for each group of four students. (Words can be repeated.) Place the stacks of cards on tables spread throughout the room. Divide the class into small groups, one for each station. Instruct each group to sit at a station. Have students pass out the word cards among themselves after you say, "Ready, set, read!" Time the round, allowing one or two minutes for students to read the word cards to each other. Then, call out "Stop!" Rotate the groups to the next table clockwise around the room by having students use some sort of controlled, aerobic movement to get there: giant stepping, crab walking, lunging, or high stepping.

Word List

after*	from*	live	soon
again*	give*	may	stop
an*	goes	now*	take
any	going*	of	thank
around	had	off	them*
as	has*	old	then*
ask*	her*	once	think*
been	him*	open	under*
by*	his*	over*	very
call	how*	please	walk*
could*	its	put*	were
don't	just	round	when*
every*	know*	said*	would
fly*	let*	some*	your*

Word is shown on the activity sheet below.

Name

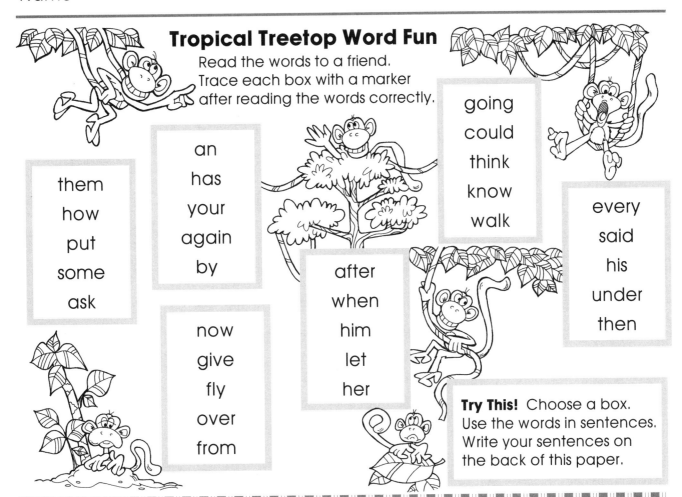

Tropical Treetop Word Fun

Read the words to a friend.
Trace each box with a marker
after reading the words correctly.

going
could
think
know
walk

an
has
your
again
by

them
how
put
some
ask

every
said
his
under
then

after
when
him
let
her

now
give
fly
over
from

Try This! Choose a box. Use the words in sentences. Write your sentences on the back of this paper.

Letter Tag

Let students play a round of the classic Freeze Tag game. Explain the rules to them if needed. One child is "It." That student runs after classmates trying to tag them. When a student has been tagged, she has to "freeze" (staying in the same position in which she was tagged). When another student crawls between a frozen player's legs, she can run around again. Once all players have been tagged, the round is over.

For the next round, tell students that whoever is It will announce a word, like *bear*. Other students run around trying to avoid being tagged. When tagged, a student becomes the new It and must say a word that starts with the next letter of the alphabet, like *camel*. Play continues as time allows and as players work through the alphabet.

Name

ABC Animal Parade

Cut out the pictures. Glue the animals in ABC order on a sheet of paper.

zebra	goat	elephant	rabbit	porcupine
horse	camel	duck	wolf	ant
fish	octopus	turtle	lion	seal

Fun, Fitness & Learning

Word Lineup in ABC Order

To play this fun word game, students will enjoy walking like animals and becoming a real-life ABC arrangement. Beforehand, make two sets of word cards by writing words on card stock: Set A is names of animals, like *anteater, baboon, cat, dog, elephant, fox, goat, hippo, jaguar, kangaroo, lion, monkey, rabbit, seal, turtle, yak,* and *zebra.* Set B is sight words.

Introduce the game by talking with students about alphabetical order and situations in which they need to use this skill. Then, divide the class into two teams and give each player a word card: Team A (animal names) and Team B (sight words). Call out an animal name and three sight words. Let players move like the designated animal and arrange themselves in ABC order using the

animal as the first word in the list. Repeat with other animal names and sight words. Play again switching teams.

Alternatively, call out two animals and six sight words for the players to sort and arrange alphabetically into two different groups.

Name _____

ABC Order Brainteaser

Cut out the words. Put them in ABC order. Then, glue the words in the boxes.

cat	fox	ostrich	tiger

going	every
eat	jump

under	please
right	white

Up & Down Letters

Invite students to search the room for upper- and lowercase letters on charts and other displays. Discuss the basic rules of when to use capital letters (names, the word *I,* first word of a sentence and so on) and show this usage in visible text. Then, divide the class in half while students are in their seats. For example, the left side of the room represents uppercase letters and the right side is the lowercase letters. Write a simple sentence without using capitals on the board or show it on a sentence strip.

they are going to see robert and josh.

Begin the game by having the Uppercase Team sitting and the Lowercase Team standing. Explain that as you read each word, if the Uppercase Team hears a word that should be capitalized they should *stand up* and the Lowercase Team should *sit down.* When the Lowercase Team hears a word that should be lowercase, they should *stand* while the other team *sits down.* Students remain in their standing or seated positions until they hear a word that causes them to make a change. Continue to show other sample sentences (being sure to use as many students' names as possible) that incorporate two or three proper nouns.

Name

Capping It Off

Finish each sentence with a word that uses a capital letter.
Write your own sentence.

_____

1. Her dog's name is _____.

_____

2. _____ likes to swim.

_____

3. Jack and _____ ran up a hill.

_____

4. _____ and I are good readers.

Ending Exercises

Introduce the activity by discussing with students how some sentences do certain jobs; they tell you something or ask a question. Point out that those sentences can either end with a period or a question mark. Then, pair students and have them write two questions and two declarative sentences on sentence strips for the game.

When the sentences are finished, have everyone do a real "exercise" using ending punctuation as the cue. Divide students into groups of four. Assign each student to be either a period or a question mark. Explain that you are going to read aloud and then display one of the prepared sentences. As you share the sentence, the students should decide what punctuation is needed:

• If the sentence should end with a period, the assigned students must do two push-ups.

• If the sentence should end with a question mark, the assigned students do three sit-ups.

Partway through the game, let students change their roles. Read aloud a variety of sentences so that students have a lot of practice thinking about ending punctuation and get their hearts pumping as well!

Alternatively, increase the challenge of the game by including exclamatory sentences. Divide the class into groups of three students and assign each student a different exercise, such as three jumping jacks for exclamation points.

Name

A Good Ending

Finish each sentence with the correct punctuation.

1. My cat takes long naps ☐

2. How old are you ☐

3. When is snack time ☐

4. She read a good book ☐

Write a telling sentence.

Write an asking sentence.

Plural Practice

Get students off their chairs and moving while thinking about nouns! First, make a set of large word cards. See the list below for possible nouns. Choose words your students can read and then write their singular and plural forms individually with large letters on card stock.

Word List

bat	cake	drum	jug	mop	rug	toy
bed	car	duck	kite	nest	shed	track
bell	cat	fan	lamp	pan	shell	trick
block	club	frog	lip	peg	shop	trip
book	cot	hat	lock	pen	sock	truck
bug	cub	hen	log	pipe	stick	tub
bus	den	hill	map	ring	tank	van
cab	dog	jet	mat	rock	tent	wing

Have students spread out in a large circle. Explain that when you call out a singular noun, they should bounce in place with their arms straight up overhead. When they recognize a plural noun, they should march in place with their hands on their hips. Then, show them the word card to reinforce what they just heard. Be sure the cards are mixed well so that students must pay attention and change exercises!

Plurals pictured on worksheet below: frogs, cars, and bugs.

Name

One or More?

Tell how many and what you see in each picture.

balls

Moving with Verb Endings

Engage your students by having them move and think about verbs. Prepare verb-ending cards -s, -ed/d, or -ing, one card for each player. On sentence strips, print simple sentences, underlining each incorrect verb, such as *Both of my dogs are run*. Form teams of three students, giving each player in the group a verb-ending card. Show a sentence. Direct the teams to determine the appropriate word ending for the underlined word. The member of each team who has the correct answer should hold up her card (-ing). The first team to show a correct answer gets to relax and choose an exercise for the other teams to perform, such as run in place for 20 seconds. If there is a tie, let everyone do a "happy dance" for 10 seconds. Sentences may include the following:

The baby is <u>crawl</u> across the floor. (*crawling*)
I <u>call</u> you yesterday. (*called*)
The bird <u>sing</u> in the tree. (*sings*)
The cars have <u>race</u> before today. (*raced*)
The man is <u>sing</u> loudly. (*singing*)
The trucks are <u>race</u> on the track. (*racing*)
The boys are <u>run</u> across the playground. (*running*)
She <u>clap</u> her hands. (*claps* or *clapped*)
The girls are <u>skip</u> over the rocks. (*skipping*)
She <u>like</u> to skip across the room. (*likes* or *liked*)
He is <u>clap</u> his hands loudly. (*clapping*)
The girl <u>jump</u> very high. (*jumps* or *jumped*)
The boy has <u>ask</u> for help. (*asked*)
The girls are <u>jump</u> over the rope. (*jumping*)
Yesterday, the bear <u>hug</u> the tree. (*hugged*)

Name

Fine Finishes

Cut out the pieces along the dashed lines.
Match the pieces to make simple sentences.
Glue them onto a sheet of paper.
On the paper, add words to make each sentence better.

The animals   The girl   The bird

The boy   The plane   The cars

race

is flying

hides

are swimming

talks

is sliding

Sentence Scramble

This sentence-building game is actually a modified relay. Gather groups of soft items, such as foam balls, in three different colors. On each of one color of item, write a simple subject (naming word), on each of another color of item write a verb (action word), and on each of the third color of item write an adjective (describing word). Plan sentences in advance so that the various parts of speech will work with a number of combinations. Write the articles *A*, *An*, and *The* on pieces of card stock and set them in the front of the room for students to use.

Place the labeled foam balls around the room in three piles, grouped by part of speech. For each round, have three players stand side by side. Then announce, "Jose, find the naming word (simple subject) of a sentence. Lamar, find an action word, and Megan, find a describing word." Direct the players to hop to the correct balls, bring their words to the front of the room, and organize them. Students should try to create a simple sentence that makes sense but perhaps is a little bit silly. Play several rounds until everyone has had a chance to hop and build sentences.

Examples include:
naming word—dog, boy, girl, cat, dinosaur
action word—ran, smiled, giggled, purred, snorted
describing word—husky, short, tall, fluffy, gigantic
articles—A, An, The

Name

Simple Sentence Story

Choose two pictures. Write a sentence about each picture that tells what you see.

Acting Out

Help students learn to recognize smaller parts of compound words with this game. Write compound words on card stock, like *beehive*, *birdbath*, *catfish*, *corncob*, *doorstop*, *fireman*, *haircut*, *lookout*, *mailbox*, *pancake*, *popcorn*, and *tugboat*. Pair students and give each team a word. Allow each student pair about a minute to demonstrate the root words of their compound word by using only hand and body gestures. Then, invite the class to try to identify it.

Extend the Lesson: Prepare the game cards by printing the words shown in the list on card stock. Divide the class into the teams, giving each group a set of cards. After students have practiced reading their words, write compound words (selected from the list on page 9) on the board. Taking turns, have students find the corresponding word parts, skip to the front of the room with their cards, and read them or act out the compound word.

Word List

Team 1	Team 2	Team 3	Team 4
cook	butter	ball	bed
horse	fire	bell	cage
light	made	boat	cat
rain	rest	room	cup
shell	sail	sick	house
step	set	tree	shoe
time	work	tug	top

Team 5	Team 6	Team 7	Team 8
back	coat	bath	bag
bird	fly	camp	cake
book	gold	foot	dog
bug	place	hand	door
day	row	man	fish
fall	sea	moon	home
tub	sun	stop	star

Name _____

Make and Match Compound Words

Cut out the pieces on the dashed lines.
Make a compound word for each picture.
Glue all of the pieces onto a sheet of paper.
Use each compound word in a sentence.
Write the sentences on your paper.

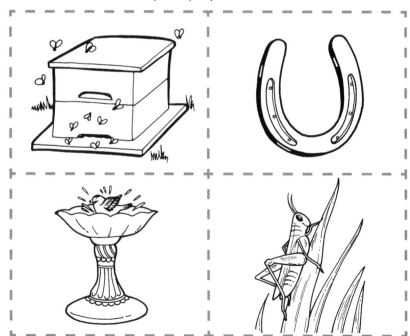

☆ bee

☆ grass

☆ horse

☆ bird

bath

hive

hopper

shoe

Shortened Words

Quick thinking about contractions is the goal of this relay game! To prepare the game "cards," ask parents to send in clean lids from margarine and whipped topping tubs. Using a permanent marker, write contractions individually on the blank surfaces of the lids. (Include other contractions that are not shown in this list if desired.) Make three game card lids for each selected contraction. Then, affix a large green dot to the top of each lid for scoring purposes.

To hide the contractions, place the sets of lids facedown in three piles at one end of the room. Divide the class into three teams and have the players stand behind the starting line at the other end of the room. Call out two words that can be shortened into a contraction. On your signal, the first student from each team walks with "baby steps" to the team's pile, searches for the matching contraction, and brings it back to the team in the same manner. The first player who returns to the starting line with the correct contraction earns a point and sets the lid down on the floor with the green dot visible. Have players take turns as you call out other words.

Word List

can't — cannot	he's — he is
didn't — did not	it's — it is
doesn't — does not	she's — she is
don't — do not	that's — that is
hadn't — had not	there's — there is
hasn't — has not	what's — what is
haven't — have not	where's — where is
wasn't — was not	who's — who is

Name _____

Understanding Contractions

Read each contraction. Write the two words used to make it.

isn't _____

what's _____

hasn't _____

she's _____

didn't _____

he's _____

that's _____

Try This! Choose **three** words below. Use each word in a sentence. Write your sentences on the back of this paper.

can't	it's
doesn't	there's
don't	wasn't
hadn't	where's
haven't	who's

Active Antonyms

Make antonyms memorable with creative actions. Select a few antonyms, print them randomly on the board, and review the words with the class. Pair students and assign each team one of the sets of antonyms. Have students incorporate those words into sentences and dramatize them for the class.

Alternatively, print antonyms on index cards. (If you need to simplify the activity, make more than one set of cards for each pair of antonyms.) Give each student a word card, making sure that the matching antonym card is held by another classmate. Allow students about one minute to move about the room attempting to act out their words until they find their matching antonyms. Repeat this activity after collecting and redistributing the cards.

Word List

bad — good	glad — sad	short — tall
big — little	go — stop	smile — frown
cold — hot	inside — outside	soft — hard
come — go	late — early	sour — sweet
dark — light	laugh — cry	sunny — cloudy
down — up	left — right	take — give
dull — bright	loud — quiet	thick — thin
early — late	new — old	to — from
enter — exit	night — day	top — bottom
fast — slow	on — off	wet — dry
few — many	open — shut	won — lost
first — last	rough — smooth	yell — whisper
found — lost	sea — land	

Name

Match the Opposites

Cut out the pieces on the dashed lines.
Match the word to its correct picture. Then, match the opposites.
Glue the pairs of antonyms onto a sheet of paper.
Use each antonym pair in a sentence. Write the sentences on your paper.

hot

sad

quiet

happy

loud

cold

Thinking of Sense-ational Words

Set up a sensory relay and have students complete the course to generate adjectives. To get started, create eight or more different stations. For the smelling stations, punch holes in containers and hide different fragrances or odors, such as cinnamon, vanilla extract, ground coffee, popped popcorn, onion, lemon juice, and sliced orange. *Follow your school's guidelines regarding the use of fragrances and inquire about students' scent sensitivities and/or allergies.* For the looking stations, find unusual items to describe. At the touching stations, place objects with different textures under towels to keep them hidden. Finally, draw on card stock a simple graphic for each station to convey to students which sense to use when observing. (See the examples of images.) Also, clearly number each station and prepare a recording sheet.

Explain to students that during their turn they will skip through the course, stopping at marked points to smell, look at, or feel certain items. Point out that as they move through each station, they must write down on their recording sheets a one-word description of what they smelled, saw, or touched. After all students have worked through the relay, invite them to share and compare the descriptive adjectives they used for each item as you reveal its identity if needed. Record the "sensational" words on chart paper.

Name

Animated Adjectives

Cut out the pieces on the dashed lines.
Match the describing words to the correct picture.
Glue the matching pieces onto a sheet of paper.
Use the phrases in sentences. Write them on your paper.

the sleek			
the sad			
the tall	boy	giraffe	baby
the tasty			
the sleepy			
the happy	cupcake	girl	cheetah

Fancy Word Face-off

Encourage students to expand their vocabularies by hosting a face-off. Divide the class into two teams. Organize the teams into two rows so that students will face one another one-on-one. Explain that you will say a word, like *sun*. Then, the first players of the teams who are facing each other must blurt out a descriptive word, like *bright*. After each student has given an acceptable answer, he must animal walk to the end of the line. The next teammate takes a turn as you present another word, such as *dog*. A student might answer, *fluffy*. Award each team one point for an acceptable response; however, if it takes more than five seconds to answer, if the descriptive word does not make sense, or if there is no guess at all, no point is given. Continue until all of the students have offered at least one good descriptive word.

Word List

apple	desk	jelly	rain	spider
bed	dog	jet	rainbow	stars
bear	doghouse	kite	ring	sun
bicycle	doormat	lamp	rock	table
bird	fish	lion	rope	tractor
butterfly	frog	parrot	seashell	tree
camera	grapes	pie	sheep	truck
cat	hair	pillow	ship	turtle
chair	hat	pizza	shirt	wagon
cheetah	helicopter	plate	snake	zebra
clock	horse	quilt	snow	
cow	ice cream	race car	sofa	

Name

Tell Me More

Finish the picture.
Write four words below to describe the water park.
On the back of this paper, write three sentences about it.

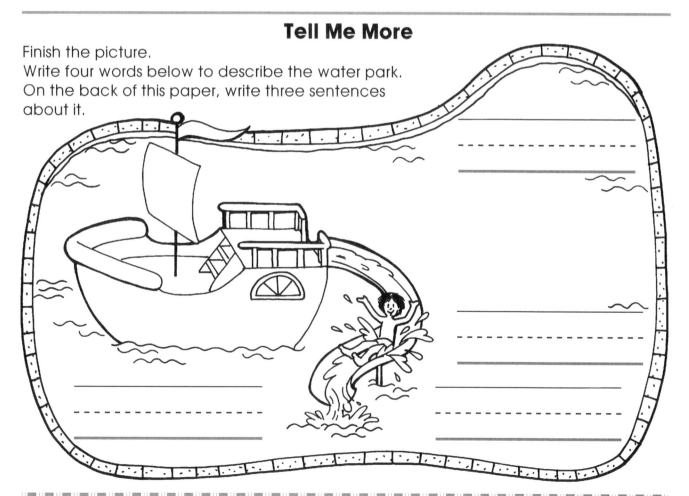

Jump-a-Thon

Counting and jumping up to 120 is easy and fun when working with a team! Divide the class into groups of four students. Give each team a jump rope and have them spread out in an open area to prevent injuries. Explain that the goal is to reach 120 jumps altogether as a team—each player contributing to the total. Player A jumps the first set of 30, Player B continues from 31 to 60, Player C does the count from 61 to 90, and Player D finishes the last set of 30 jumps.

To build endurance, reduce the number of members on a team and have them repeat the steps and jump a total of 120 times. When your students are ready to work individually and jump nonstop (up to 120 times), provide each child with a jump rope and see if a record can be set. Be sure to celebrate this jumping-while-counting feat in a special way!

Name

Write the numbers 1–60 in the boxes.

1									
							18		
				25					
	32								
			44						
					57				

Try This! Keep on counting. Write the numbers 61–120 on a sheet of paper.

In Perfect Order

Work with "green" numbers by reusing milk cartons (individual serving size). Collect 31 clean, empty milk cartons and tape them closed. Write numbers (0–30) on pieces of card stock using a green permanent marker. Affix a number to each carton by covering it with clear packing tape.

Place four or five piles of cartons in the middle of the room. Let players from teams take turns racing to a pile and arranging the cartons in numerical order. Change the assortment of numbers in the piles for each round of play.

As you collect and prepare more milk cartons, build your set of numbered items up to 100 or 120. Then, raise the difficulty level of the game.

Variations:

- Have students select a specified quantity of cartons randomly and arrange those numbers in numerical order (e.g., 51, 63, 76, 84, . . .).
- Leave out certain numbers in the pile and have students arrange all of the remaining cartons numerically.

Repeat the game many times in different ways to build number sense up to 120!

Name

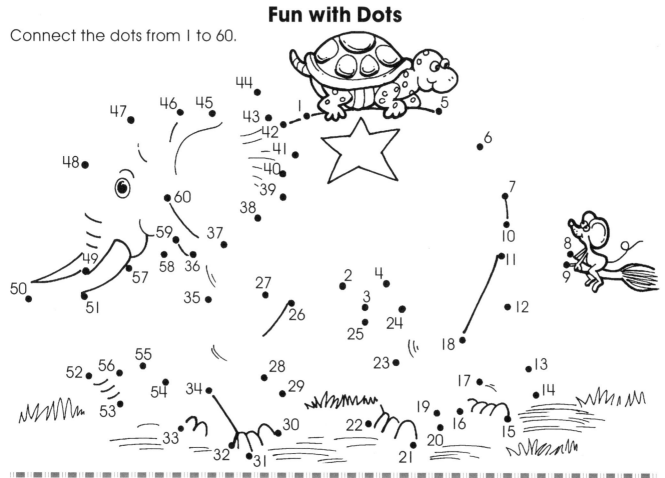

Fun with Dots

Connect the dots from 1 to 60.

31

A Greater Game

Divide the class into two teams. Have each team stand in two separate lines about 15 feet (4.5 m) apart and facing each other. In between the two teams, place a soft object, such as a pillow, which is to be the "bait." Assign each student on each team a number from 5 to 30. Be sure to give both teams the same set of numbers. Explain that when you call out a number problem, like "It is greater than 10 (pause) but less than 12," the student on each team with that assigned number races for the bait. The one who brings it back to his side without being tagged by the opposing player earns a point for his team. However, if he gets tagged, no one gets the point. The first team to earn the predetermined number of points wins the game.

Name _____

More or Less?

Use the greater than (>) and less than (<) symbols to fill in the math sentences.
Cut out and glue them in the correct boxes.

____ is greater than ____	____ is less than ____

8 _____ 1	12 _____ 31	73 _____ 67
45 _____ 46	28 _____ 18	43 _____ 52

All Mixed Up!

Engage your young learners with this build-and-show numbers game. Prepare single-digit cards (0–9) in two different colors (e.g., red and blue) on card stock. Scatter the cards faceup throughout the room. Let students position themselves among the numeral cards. Announce a color and a certain number, such as 52. The students standing closest to the corresponding digit cards (5 and 2) in the correct color should find each other, hop to the front of the room with the cards, and display them for the class. Continue the game with other numbers.

Alternatively, reinforce place value for numbers up to 100 by building and showing numbers in two ways. Assemble 20 bundles of 10 craft sticks that have been secured with rubber bands. Set 10 bundles (wrapped with red yarn) along with nine loose craft sticks on a tabletop and also place 10 bundles (wrapped with blue yarn) with nine craft sticks on another table. Scatter the digit cards on the floor throughout the room. Divide the class into two teams. Have Team A members stand around the room near the digit cards. Let Team B members stand near one of the tables. Announce a color (red or blue) and a certain number. Team players should hop to the front of the room with digit cards or craft sticks to show the given number to earn a point for their teams.

Name

To the Teacher: Have the child circle each group of ten if needed.

"Shapely" Numbers

Count the groups of ten and ones. Write the number in each box.

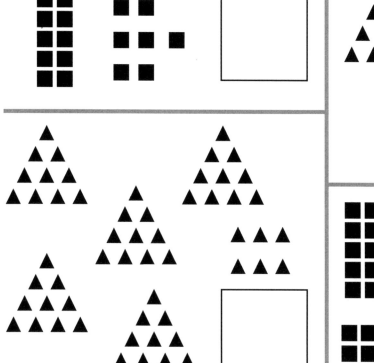

Try This! Write the given numbers in order from smallest to largest on the back of this paper.

Balloon Bop or Pass!

Blow up several balloons (not latex) in two different colors. *Follow your school's guidelines regarding the use of balloons in the classroom.* Using a permanent marker, number each balloon with a different number. Then, write the same numbers separately on pieces of card stock. Place each set of colored balloons in a large trash bag on the floor. Divide the class into two teams and have them stand single file behind the starting line. Briefly review the math concepts of "equal to," "greater than," and "less than" with the students. Let the first player for each team skip (walk backwards, hop, or slide) to the team's bag to get a balloon and then skip back with it to the starting line.

Show the teams a number. Each player must determine if her chosen numbered balloon is . . .

- **Greater than your number**—Player must go down the line batting the balloon to each team member who then bats it back to the player.
- **Less than your number**—The balloon is passed between the legs of the team members *two* times.
- **Equal to your number**—Player must bop the balloon in the air while walking around the room.

Name

Dare to Compare

Count the animals. Draw more animals and write the math sentence.

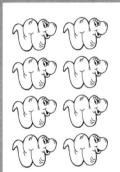

is greater than

10 > ____

is less than

____ ____ ____

is less than

____ ____ ____

is equal to

____ ____ ____

Quick Counting

For this moving-to-count game, all you need are large quantities of small objects. Set up counting areas throughout the classroom by placing a variety of similar objects in containers at each station: larger-sized items (small balls, miniature toy cars, beanbags) and smaller-sized items (dice, dried beans, linking cubes, paper clips, seashells, and colored pasta shapes). On each container, indicate how students should group and count the items. For larger objects like balls, have them skip count by 2s, but for the smaller items, have them group the items together and count by 5s or 10s.

Pair students and give each team a recording sheet for the work stations. Instruct the teams to skip from station to station and count the objects in each container. Have students record their answers on the paper. When the counting is finished, let students compare their answers with yours.

Name _____

Skip to My Two (and Five and Ten)!

Start counting at 0 (zero) and color in the correct boxes.
1. Skip count by **10s** and color each box **red**.
2. Skip count by **5s** and draw stripes (///) in each box.
3. Skip count by **2s** and color each box **blue**.

									0
1	2	3	4	5	6	7	8	9	10
11	12	13	14	15	16	17	18	19	20
21	22	23	24	25	26	27	28	29	30
31	32	33	34	35	36	37	38	39	40
41	42	43	44	45	46	47	48	49	50
51	52	53	54	55	56	57	58	59	60
61	62	63	64	65	66	67	68	69	70
71	72	73	74	75	76	77	78	79	80
81	82	83	84	85	86	87	88	89	90
91	92	93	94	95	96	97	98	99	100

Estimation Station

Set up the classroom so that there are only work stations in the open area. Move the chairs out of the way. On each table or desktop, place a covered, clear plastic container that holds several small- or medium-sized items, such as dry beans, dice, or wooden blocks. Or, in the station, place a pile of objects, like calculators. *To help first graders make better estimates at each station, include a comparison container or pile of objects that has been labeled with its quantity.* Prepare a recording sheet for students to use when estimating.

Pair students and have them spread throughout the room, each one armed with a pencil and a recording sheet. Direct students to tiptoe throughout the room, stopping at each table and recording their best guess of how many items are in the mystery container or pile. Use a timer and announce when students should tiptoe to different stations. Allow students to move around to each station twice so that they can evaluate and, if needed, adjust their estimations. Finally, gather the students around each station and together count the objects in each container or pile so that they can see how accurately they estimated.

Name

To the Teacher: If the child wants to color the balls, provide a color pencil.

Almost Math

Estimate how many objects you see. Then, touch each thing with a crayon and count your marks.

How many cell phones?

Estimate: _____   Count: _____

How many balls?

Estimate: _____   Count: _____

How many ✳ ?

Estimate: _____

Count: _____

Try This!
On the back of this paper, draw many pizza slices, blocks, or butterflies. Have your friend estimate how many you drew and then count them.

2, 4, 6, 8, Skip Counting Sure Is Great!

Rework the original "Two, Four, Six, Eight" number rhyme and incorporate higher numbers and additional skip-counting choices. Share the original rhyme with the class. Then, teach students the new verses for skip-counting rhymes as they jump rope or perform fun actions.

Two, four, six, eight,
Counting by twos sure is great!
Ten, twelve, fourteen, sixteen,
Come on, guys, use your bean!
Eighteen, twenty, twenty-two, twenty-four,
Oh, I bet you want some more!

Five, ten, fifteen, twenty,
Want some more, we've got plenty!
Twenty-five, thirty, thirty-five, forty,
Counting by fives sure sounds sporty!
Forty-five, fifty, fifty-five, sixty,
Hey, that sounds almost nifty!

Ten, twenty, thirty, forty,
Count some more, don't leave 'em, shorty!
Fifty, sixty, seventy, eighty,
Keep it moving, ahoy there, matey!
Ninety, one hundred, got another number?
Sure, we do, but it's time to slumber.

For an added challenge and good
introduction to skip counting by threes, also
teach the following verse:

Three, six, nine, twelve,
Now we're just starting to delve!
Fifteen, eighteen, twenty-one, twenty-four,
Counting by threes is not even a chore!
Twenty-seven, thirty, thirty-three, thirty-six,
We go fast with these number tricks!

Add-a-Rep

Here's a fun way to generate addition equations. Pair students and let them stand in an open area. Be sure each student team has a pencil and scratch paper. Explain that you are going to lead students in a variety of exercises, but for each round only one student in each pair will participate. For example, begin by leading Player A of each team in jumping jacks for seven or eight seconds. Have those students record how many jumping jacks they completed on the scratch paper. Then, lead the other half of the teams in jumping jacks for four seconds and have them record how many they completed. Stop so that the pairs can work together to add how many jumping jacks they completed altogether. Continue to lead students in a variety of exercises to boost addition skills and let them expend a lot of energy.

Name _____

It All Adds Up!

Draw the missing animals. Write the answer in the blank.

$6 + $ _____ $= 10$ penguins

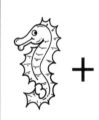

$1 + $ _____ $= 10$ sea horses

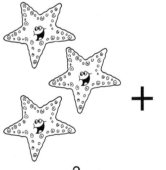

$3 + $ _____ $= 10$ starfish

$8 + $ _____ $= 10$ sharks

Try This! On the back of this paper, draw objects to show the problem $5 + $ ___ $= 10$.

Equation Invasion

For this relay, divide students into four teams. Have each team line up single file behind an empty basket that has been placed on the starting line. Assign a captain for each team as the runner. Set four tubs of soft foam balls directly across the room from the starting line. Explain that after you have announced the addition problem, the first student (Player A) of each team will pick up the basket, walk with giant steps to the tub of balls, and gather the correct number of balls to complete the given equation, such as 3 + 2 = __. She must walk back with giant steps to the starting line with the basket. When the four players have returned with their selections, check the quantities to see if they are correct and award points to teams. Give one point to each team who collects the correct number of balls and give an extra point to the

player who returned first. The captains keep track of the scores and carry the foam balls back to the tubs after each round of play. The game is continued as Player B in each line takes a turn. Repeat the steps until all players, except the captains, have run the addition relay. Then, let students celebrate by tossing the balls into the baskets from various distances.

Alternatively, have students solve missing addend problems, such as 3 + __ = 5.

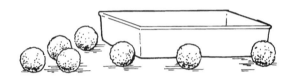

Name

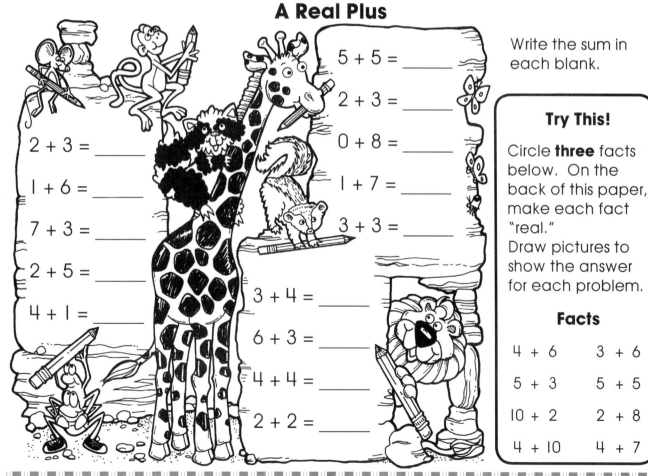

A Real Plus

Write the sum in each blank.

2 + 3 = _____

1 + 6 = _____

7 + 3 = _____

2 + 5 = _____

4 + 1 = _____

5 + 5 = _____

2 + 3 = _____

0 + 8 = _____

1 + 7 = _____

3 + 3 = _____

3 + 4 = _____

6 + 3 = _____

4 + 4 = _____

2 + 2 = _____

Try This!

Circle **three** facts below. On the back of this paper, make each fact "real."
Draw pictures to show the answer for each problem.

Facts

4 + 6	3 + 6
5 + 3	5 + 5
10 + 2	2 + 8
4 + 10	4 + 7

Sneaky Subtraction

For this subtraction game, set up eight stations on tables or desktops around the room. Gather eight small boxes with lids (pencil boxes work well) and label them individually with letters *A–H*. Place several of the same type of common objects, such as small toys, markers, plastic spoons, etc., in each box. Prepare a recording sheet for students to use.

Divide the class into teams of two or three students. Instruct them to move from station to station in a clockwise manner around the room and record the number of items in each box. When they have finished the work, let students march (high stepping) around the room while chanting the rhyme "Count Back!" Repeat the rhyme as needed until everyone has walked around the classroom. While the students are marching, secretly

remove some items from each box. Then, have students return to each station and count the items that remain and record the number.

Finally, direct students to use the given numbers to create subtraction problems, like "8 pencils – 2 pencils = 6 pencils." As a class, review each station's math problem so that students can check their work and find out what you slipped into your pockets!

Count Back!
Twelve, eleven, ten, nine,
Counting backwards sure is fine!
Eight, seven, six, five,
Come on, guys, let's do the jive!
Four, three, two, one,
Yes, we're ready for "take away" FUN!

- -

Name

What's Left in the Chest?

Draw coins or gems to show how many are left in the chest. Fill in the blank.

8 – 2 = _____ coins

9 – 4 = _____ gems

7 – 5 = _____ gems

10 – 3 = _____ coins

Try This! On the back of this paper, make up **two** math problems for a friend to solve.

Stand & Sit Subtraction

Let students think and move their bodies when working with subtraction. Divide the class into three teams and direct them to move their chairs close together. Have students begin this activity by standing in front of their chairs so that the back of their knees meet the seats (making it safer for standing up and sitting down quickly). Explain that you are going to call out a subtraction problem for all of the players to solve. If the players think the answer is greater than five, they should stand up. If the answer is five or less, they should sit down. Award two points to each team that has all of its players indicating the correct answer. Give one point to a team if a few of its players made the correct decision. Continue with more rounds of problems, each time recording scores with tally marks on the board, until one of the teams reaches a predetermined total to win the game.

Game Problems

Team 1	Team 2	Team 3
4–3	10–5	8–2
9–4	5–3	10–4
7–5	9–0	9–6
10–2	7–6	8–3
9–8	8–1	10–7
10–1	9–9	9–1
8–4	6–5	8–6
10–8	10–3	6–4
7–1	9–5	10–9
9–2	6–2	8–5
6–3	10–6	6–1
9–3	7–7	7–2

Name

Spectacular Subtraction

Solve. Trace the circle to show the correct answer.

4 – 3 = ③ ① ⑤

5 – 2 = ③ ⑦ ⑨

7 – 1 = ① ⑧ ⑥

9 – 4 = ⑤ ④ ⑬

10 – 3 = ⑧ ⑬ ⑦

More to Solve!

12 – 2 = ⑩ ⑭ ⑪

14 – 1 = ⑫ ⑪ ⑬

13 – 3 = ⑪ ⑩ ⑫

11 – 2 = ⑦ ⑧ ⑨

15 – 2 = ⑫ ⑬ ⑭

Fraction Action

Let students move about the room to demonstrate fractions in action! First, explain how you are going to use the class itself to teach about fractions. Begin the lesson by having all of the students (if there is an even number of students) stand very close together in the middle of an open space. Tell them that this is one whole class. Then, point out half of the class and have those students hop to one side of the room. Direct the other half of the class to hop to the opposite side of the room. Explain that each side equals one-half of the whole group. Write $\frac{1}{2}$ on the board. Direct students to crawl back to the center of the room and stand close together. Once again, explain that now they are a whole group. Write $\frac{1}{1}$ on the board. Next, ask the class to divide in half and hop to designated locations again.

Point out half of each divided group and have them hop to another area of the room to make four groups. Explain that four equal groups have been created, each equaling one-fourth of the entire class. Write $\frac{1}{4}$ on the board. Let students crawl back together to form a whole group. Continue the demonstration as needed.

Name

Fun with Fractions

Divide each shape. Show **2 equal parts**. Color one-half ($\frac{1}{2}$) of each shape.

Divide each shape. Show **4 equal parts**.

Color one-fourth ($\frac{1}{4}$) of each shape.

Circle to show equal shares of a group.

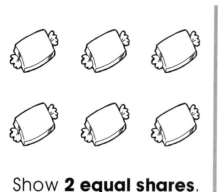

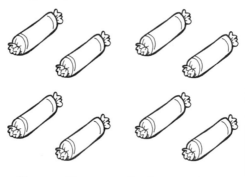

Show **2 equal shares**.

Show **4 equal shares**.

Show **1 whole group**.

Coin Counting

Use the tune of "One Little, Two Little, Three Little ____" to help children remember how many dimes and how many nickels equal a dollar. Choose 10 students to represent dimes and give each one a coin (10¢) drawn on card stock. Direct the chosen students to squat down like frogs side by side, holding their paper coins. Assign each student a number 1–10. Explain that as the class sings the song, each student with a coin must pop up when he hears his number. (Number 10 jumps up on the words "ten dimes.") Sing a few full rounds having different students hold the coins each time.

To reinforce the number of nickels that equal a dollar, make 20 paper nickels for students to hold. Pair students and number each group, counting by 2s up to 20. Then, have the students march (high stepping) around the room

with their coins while singing the second verse. As each number is sung, the corresponding pair of students raise their paper coins above their heads. Keep on marching until all of the nickels are lifted up and then stop to cheer with a rousing "Hooray!"

One Little, Two Little, Three Little Coins

One little, two little, three little dimes,
Four little, five little, six little dimes,
Seven little, eight little, nine little dimes,
Collect ten dimes for a dollar. HOORAY! *(Cheer loudly.)*

Two little, four little, six little nickels,
Eight little, ten little, twelve little nickels,
Fourteen little, sixteen little, eighteen little nickels,
Show twenty nickels for a dollar. HOORAY!

- -

Name

To the Teacher: Draw or stamp dimes and nickels in the boxes to program the activity.

Count the value of the coins. Write the amount in the blank.

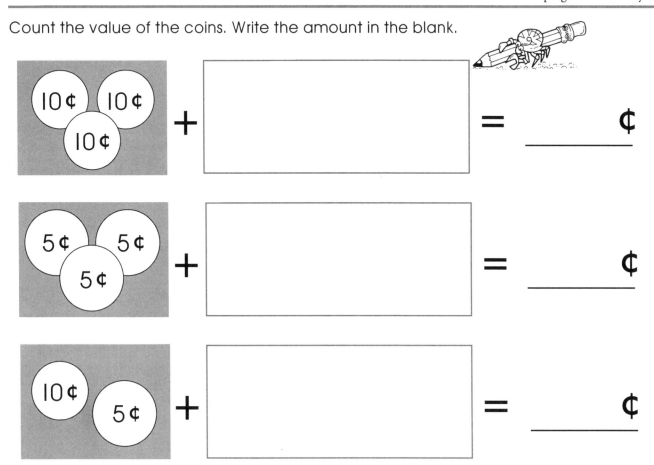

Try this! Draw **three** money problems on the back of this paper for a friend to solve.

Predictable Patterns

Set up a fun predictable obstacle course indoors with at least six physical challenges that follow a basic alternating pattern, like ABAB. You could have students crawl under a table, stop and spin around two times on a mat, crawl under another table, stop and spin around two times on a mat, and so on. After each student has completed the short course, have the class predict what should happen next to continue the pattern.

Create a variety of obstacle courses, making each path follow a different but predictable pattern, such as ABC, by adding a straddle jump over a pillow or a forward roll on carpet squares or hopping with both feet together over a row of stuffed animals. Have students line up in single file so that they can

take their turns individually; however, keep the action going. Follow up the activity by discussing the variety of patterns the students completed. Let them suggest a new course for a repeating pattern, such as ACC, ABAC, AABB, ABDD, or ABCDE. Remember to use the same physical challenge each time to represent a certain letter, such as *A* stands for crawl under a table, *B* stands for stop and spin around two times on a mat, *C* stands for straddle jump over a pillow, and so on to reinforce the concept.

Alternatively, assign a different physical challenge for each letter and let students create new courses.

Name

What Is Next?

Cut out each strip. Glue strips onto a sheet of paper. Draw more objects to continue each pattern. Name each repeating pattern using numbers or letters, such as ABAB.

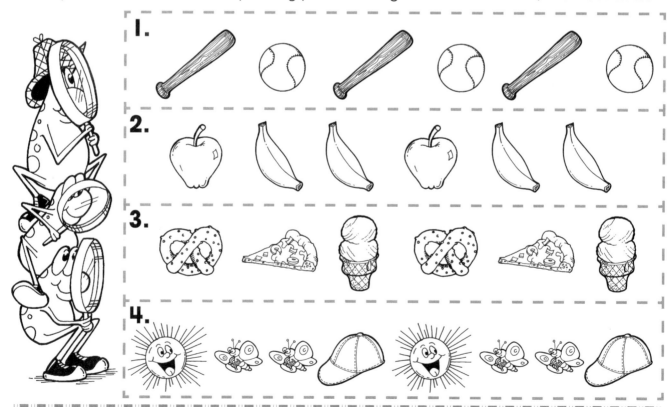

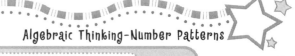

Detecting the Rule

Take a "milk break" with skip counting! Gather clean milk cartons and label them with numbers (0–120) or use the ones prepared for the activity "In Perfect Order." (See page 31.) Set up four areas with milk cartons and divide the class into teams for the stations. Give cartons 0–30 to Team A, cartons 31–60 to Team B, cartons 61–90 to Team C, and cartons 91–120 to Team D. Start a number pattern by calling out the following numbers: 6, 16, 26. Let Team A players lunge step to the front of the room with those cartons. Then, have three players

from each of the other teams bring the cartons needed to continue the pattern by walking with lunge steps as well. If the numbers are correct, have Team A tell you the "jump rule" you used. If not correct, direct the players to return to their stations for the right cartons. Continue the game by announcing other series of numbers. After three rounds of play, rotate the students to different stations so that Team A players become Team B, Team B players become Team C, and so on.

Name _____

To the Teacher: Have the child work with fewer number strips if needed.

Jumping Up to 100

- Look at each number sequence. How large is each jump? Write the number in the blank on the rule strip.
- Cut out each strip.
- Match each rule to a number strip. Glue them onto a sheet of paper.
- Tell what's next. Count and write the numbers up to 100 for each strip.

Jump by ____	0	10	20	30	40
Jump by ____	25	30	35	40	45
Jump by ____	25	35	45	55	65
Jump by ____	13	23	33	43	53

Sorting Stations

Grouping objects by common attributes can be a fun, logical task! Set up small sorting stations around the room by placing collections of objects on desks or tabletop areas. Plan each work station so that students can sort the items into two or three groups, using criteria such as shape, size, or color. The collection of objects stored in a box at each station can include a variety of small- to medium-sized items, like pencils, paper clips, math manipulatives, etc.

Pair students and have them choose a station. After they sort their items and return them to the box, direct students to hop to a different station. Let students continue to travel around the room so that they can gain practice thinking logically about objects.

Name

Sort Report

Cut out the pictures. Sort them by kind of object. Then, sort them into **2 groups**.

Fun with Fitness & Math

Get your class moving with this data collecting activity! Explain to students that they are going to do a 15-second challenge. Pair students so that they can take turns being the "counter." Demonstrate an exercise, such as running in place, jumping jacks, hopping on one foot, straddle toe touches, or walking across the room with lunges. Then, watch the time as Player A of each team tries to complete as many as repetitions possible. Have students record their scores using tally marks on scrap paper. Then, let Player B of each team perform the exercise. Continue the challenge until all of the students have completed three different exercises.

Collect all of the numbers to make a class graph on the white board or chart paper. Students will enjoy seeing the large totals!

After doing some tallying and graphing as a large group, provide each pair of students with a copy of the activity sheet below. Get them started by brainstorming together possible questions they could ask classmates, such as questions about favorite sports to play or favorite outdoor activities. Guide students through each step.

Name _____

To the Teacher: Enlarge the grid for the student if needed.

Tallyho and Graphing Go!

- Cut out the grid and glue it onto a sheet of paper.
- Think of a question to ask your classmates.
- Use tally marks to record their answers on that paper.
- Then, make a bar graph of that information. Use the grid.
- Label the parts of your graph.

17
16
15
14
13
12
11
10
9
8
7
6
5
4
3
2
1
0

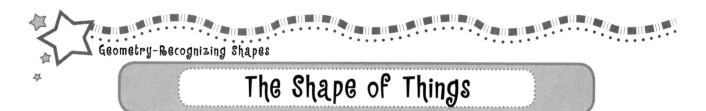
The Shape of Things

Practice reading shape words and recognizing the geometric shapes of actual objects with this activity. Copy the provided shapes on card stock and cut them apart. Laminate the cards for durability if desired. Place a low table in the middle of the room. Scatter around the room a variety of objects representing different two- and three-dimensional shapes: square, circle, rectangle, triangle, oval, trapezoid, rhombus, cube, cone, cylinder, rectangular prism, and sphere. Include as many real-world objects as possible.

Shapes may include:
• circle— rubber band, CD, school play money
• oval—picture frame, serving tray, plastic egg
• rectangle—domino, small student board, sheet of notebook paper, serving tray
• square—ceramic tile, geoboard, cutting board
• triangle—music instrument, pennant

• cone—birthday party hat, funnel, cone for sports
• cube—bead, wooden letter block
• cylinder—empty can, spool of thread, battery, bead
• rectangular prism—facial tissue box, small pencil sharpener, battery
• sphere—ball (any size), bead, globe, grapefruit

Also incorporate pattern blocks, solid geometric shapes, and other math manipulatives in the collection of samples.

Have students gather together in the middle of the room around the table and sit on the floor. Call out the name of a shape for each pair of students. Have each team find the corresponding shape card and a related object in the room to make a match. Continue the game as time and interest allow.

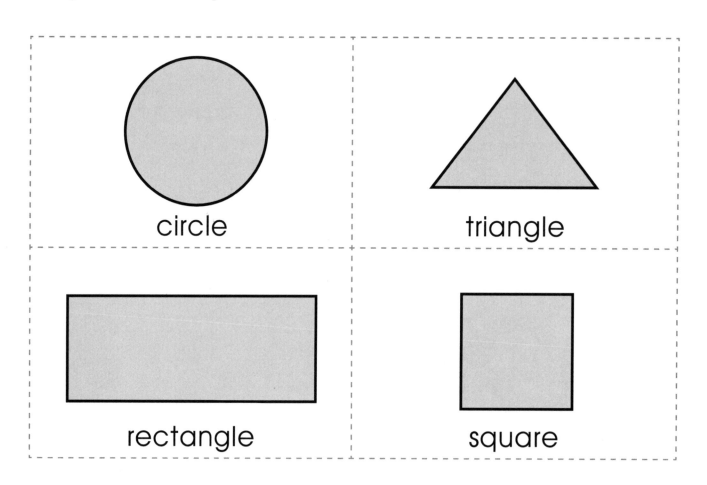

circle

triangle

rectangle

square

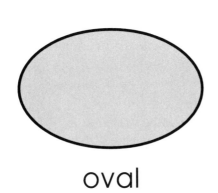

oval

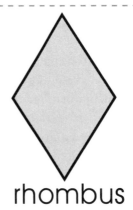

rhombus

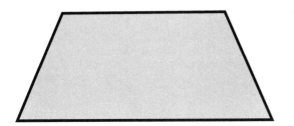

trapezoid

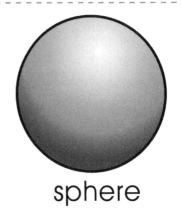

sphere

cone

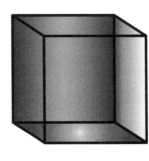

cube

cylinder

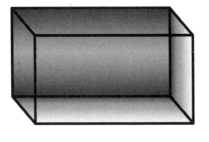

rectangular prism

Going to Long Lengths

Teach students about measuring the length of objects by having them be the "tools." Start the investigation by asking, "How many first graders long is this classroom?" To find out, have students lie down, foot to head, the length of the room to measure it. Then, have them estimate how many first graders wide the classroom is. Take students throughout the school to determine various dimensions of spaces, such as the school gymnasium and media center. Finish by measuring the playground and its equipment, such as the length of the slide "in first graders" for a fun playtime reward.

Name _____

Moving to Measure!

- Number the squares (1–14) at the bottom of the page.
- Find an object that matches each length. Color the star when found.
- Show a friend the objects.

Look for something . . .

 10 squares long

 14 squares long

 5 squares long

 3 squares long

 8 squares long

 This is _____ squares long.

Hands Above the Rest

Introduce the basic concepts of telling time to the hour and half hour with actions! Have students spread throughout the room at least an arm length apart. Stand in front of the class and demonstrate various times on an analog clock with your arms. Straighten one arm to represent the long (or hour) hand and bend the other arm to demonstrate the short (or minute) hand. Have students mimic your actions as you demonstrate various clock times, such as 6 o'clock, 7 o'clock, half past 8 or 8:30, and so on. Be sure to explain clearly the purpose of the hour hand and the minute hand for telling the hour and half-hour times. Finally, write various times on the board to see if students can show the times using their arms without a clock model.

Alternatively, when your students understand the movements of the hour and minute hands, change the activity into a game. Divide the class into four or five teams. Have the teams stand single file behind the starting line. On your signal, let the first player in line high step to the front of the room, turn to face the team, and pretend to be clocks. Call out a time for those players to show with their arms and award a point to each team if the demonstration is correct. Let those players high step back to the end of the lines. Then, have the second players step right up to show more clock action. Continue the game as time and interest allow.

- -

Name

To the Teacher: Program the watches/boxes and the start time before copying the sheet.

Watch the Time!

Show the time on the watch or in the box.

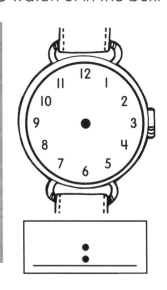

Try This!
Look at the clock. If you play outside for two hours, at what time will you stop?

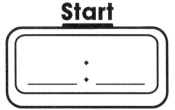
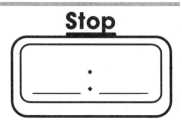

Blooming Science

As a class, brainstorm a list of various plants (tall trees, garden flowers, trailing vines, etc.). Then, have students "become" many of the different kinds of plants described. Begin by instructing students to spread throughout the room, allowing plenty of space between them. Lead the class in a series of yoga-like stretches as they start as tiny seeds, grow roots and stems, and blossom into mature plants. As you and the students form each type of plant, be sure to point out the key parts, such as the seed, roots, leaf, and flower/fruit. Also, talk about basic plant needs—water, air, and light—and incorporate any other key plant terms you are studying.

Name

Plant Parts

Label the parts of the pumpkin plant. Color the picture.

Vocabulary	flower	leaf
	roots	stem

Animal Antics

Here's a fun search-and-sort activity for engaging your budding scientists. Make enlarged copies of the animal pictures on this page and on page 54 or create your own paper cutout shapes of animals. Hide the prepared pictures or shapes throughout the room. Be sure to include a variety of mammals, birds, and fish, as well as some other kinds of animals that do not fit the criteria.

Gather students and explain the search. Let them look all over the room for "animals" while walking on tiptoes so that the creatures will not be "spooked"! When a student finds an animal, he should attach it to a bulletin board display in the corresponding category, such as habitat or according to classification.

Then, he must "act" like the animal while circling the room to celebrate his find. Continue until all of the animals have been found.

Name

What Kind?

Cut out the pictures and labels. Sort the animals into the correct groups.
Glue everything on a large sheet of paper to show the groups.

Mammals	Fish
Birds	Other Animals

53

Stone Sort

Gather different rocks, having them vary in color, shape, texture, or size. Place an equal number of rocks in three different pails and then set each container in a different area of the room. Divide the class into three groups and have them stand together, side by side. Tell the groups that they first must make a decision about how they will sort their rocks (color, shape, texture, or size). Then, give the signal and let the first person from each team slide (side step) up to a designated pail, select a rock, and place it on the floor or ground. She then slides back to her team and touches the next player's hand. That player takes off to select another rock from the pail. This relay continues until each team has sorted all of its rocks by likeness. Students will have to work together—as well as be accurate—to complete the task.

Name _____

To the Teacher: Have the child tell a friend how the stones are alike.

Stone Studying

Find three stones. Tape each stone to the middle of a square.
Then, compare the stones. Write a few words to tell how each one is different.

Stone A	Stone B	Stone C

Stone A _____

_____

Stone B _____

_____

Stone C _____

_____

Weather Workout

Gather the class in the afternoon and have them make a prediction about the weather conditions for the following day. If you fill in a weather calendar each day, place a weather symbol on it to show your prediction as well. Have students complete their copies of the weather watch chart shown below.

At the beginning of each day, ask students to share their predictions. Let those who correctly predicted the weather conditions choose and lead the entire class in a simple exercise, such as 30 jumping jacks. Also, include a movement to indicate the actual weather conditions for the day. Be sure to join your students' workout based on your own weather guesses, too. This should energize everyone for a busy day of learning!

Here are some ideas for movements and exercises:

• Rainstorm—Run in place for one minute (to sound like thunder); touch toes 10 times (lightning strikes).

• Light rain shower—Pat thighs for 30 seconds.

• Windy day—Extend arms out from the sides of the body. Raise one arm above the head while dropping the other arm down towards the floor to stretch the trunk. Then, change the direction of the arms. Repeat 10 times.

• Sunny day—Extend arms out to the sides. Twist the trunk gently back and forth (10 times) to move one arm in front of the body and one behind it.

• Snowy day—Raise extended arms above the head. Wiggle fingers while moving the arms down in front of the body. Repeat 5 times.

Name _____

To the Teacher: For the temperature scale, print *F* or *C* before copying the sheet.

Weather Watch

• Guess what the weather will be like the next day. Do this for one week.
• Draw a "weather symbol" to show your prediction.
• Color the star if you made a good prediction.
• During the actual day, find out the air temperature. Record it below.

Monday	Tuesday	Wednesday	Thursday	Friday
☆	☆	☆	☆	☆

Go Get It Globe!

Go Get It Globe! is a fun game that can be played two different ways. First, prepare the materials by enlarging and copying the patterns for the seven continent shapes (which have been simplified) on card stock and then cut out the pieces. Laminate the shapes for durability. Using a hot glue gun (if the shapes are laminated), attach a piece of a hook-and-loop tape on the blank side of each paper continent. On a wall, post a large blue felt shape (which has been cut to look like a flattened Earth) and arrange matching hook-and-loop tape pieces in the corresponding locations.

Have students form seven groups and stand behind a designated spot on the floor. Give the first person in each group a continent game piece. Have those players skip (high step, lunge, gallop, side step/slide, etc.) to the blue "Earth" on the wall and attach their game pieces. When the seven pieces are arranged correctly,

the entire class should chant "You got it!" (four times). Then, the next player in each group skips to the wall, retrieves the continent piece placed by a team member, and hands it to you while naming it, e.g., "This is Antarctica." Continue the game in the same manner by giving the third player of each team a different game piece to display on blue Earth. To extend the learning, slowly add the names of major oceans and include them with the continent shapes when your students are ready for a new challenge.

Game Variation: Tape the paper continent shapes on a beach ball to make a classroom "Got It Globe!" Toss the prepared ball around the room. Each student who catches the "globe" must name the continent that is nearest to or being touched by the thumb on the left hand. The student then tosses the ball to someone else. Continue the game as time and interest allow.

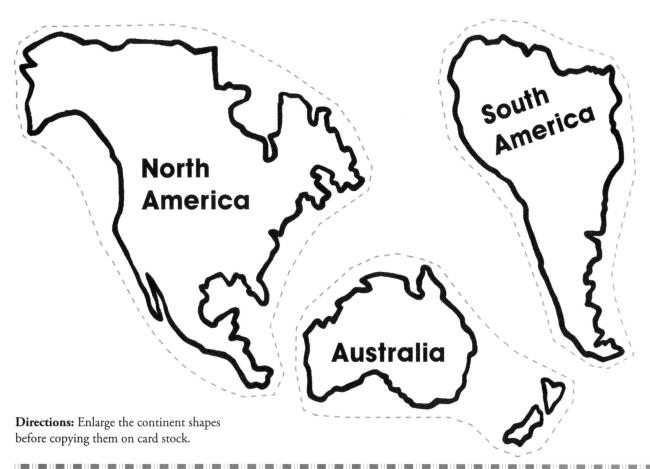

Directions: Enlarge the continent shapes
before copying them on card stock.

Directions: Enlarge the continent shapes before copying them on card stock.

Movin' with Maps

Introduce your students to maps by having them read one that is prepared by you. First, create a basic map showing the main parts of the school building along with the location of your classroom. Make several copies of the map. On each copy, write a different set of directions for a group of students to read so that they must use arrows and landmarks on the designated path to navigate back to the classroom.

Divide the class into teams of two or three students and give each one a prepared map. Depending on the size of your school's campus, it may be beneficial to have parent or school volunteers posted in key areas throughout the building or accompany student teams as needed. Once each team has returned to the room,

celebrate their happy returns and good map-reading skills with healthy snacks.

Name

My Map

Think about your neighborhood.
Draw a map to show what is there.

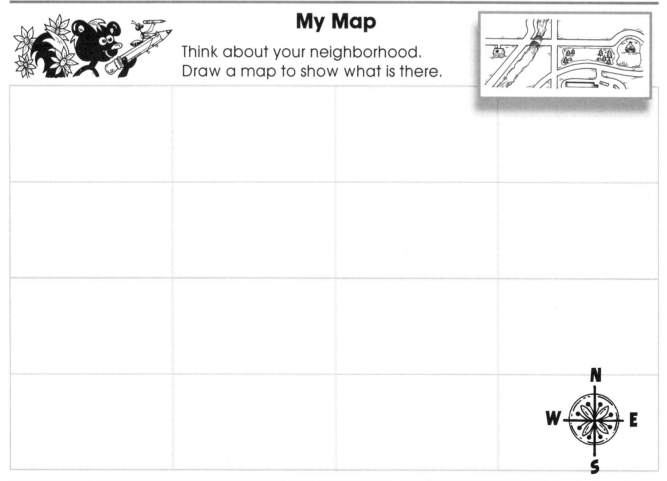

The Rules Rule!

Set up a class obstacle course by placing several safe barriers on the floor, such as empty plastic containers and pillows. Remove all tables and any other hard objects from the playing area. Demonstrate the course for students; then, explain that they are going to work as a democracy to form the laws (rules) for how to complete the course. Encourage them to think as a true democracy by showing fairness and considering the safety of themselves and the other citizens (their classmates). Some sample rules might include the following:

- Only one player at a time on the course
- No talking when someone is doing the course

After students feel confident that the laws will keep all of them happy and safe, allow them to have fun and navigate through the course!

Name

Make a list of rules at your school.

Rules at School

_____

- -

_____

- -

_____

- -

_____

- -

_____

Patriotic Parade

Gather the class together for a discussion on what it means to be a good citizen. Point out that you can be a citizen (or member) of many groups, like a household, neighborhood, community, or country. Explain that citizens have responsibilities when they are in a group. For example, they must follow the laws. Also show and discuss pictures of national symbols and songs, such as the flag, the nation's important buildings, the pledge, the national anthem, and so on.

Wrap up the lesson by providing students with a variety of craft materials so that each student can make a model of an important national symbol or flag. Supply large craft sticks as handles for the paper symbols. Conduct a class parade throughout the school, proudly marching and singing patriotic songs. For U.S. citizens, stop periodically to recite the pledge for "parade onlookers."

Name

Wonderful Words

Tell why you think your country is special.
Add some details to the flag.

I think my country is special because . . .

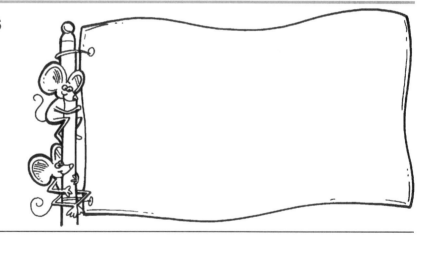

Social Studies

Standards Correlations

First Grade Fun, Fitness & Learning supports the National Association for Sport and Physical Education's (NASPE) *Moving into the Future: National Standards for Physical Education* and the National Council of Teachers of English (NCTE) and the International Reading Association (IRA) *Standards for the English Language Arts.* This resource also supports the National Council of Teachers of Mathematics (NCTM) *Principles and Standards for School Mathematics,* the National Council for the Social Studies (NCSS) *National Curriculum Standards for Social Studies,* and the *National Science Education Standards.*

····· NASPE *Moving into the Future: National Standards for Physical Education* ·····

This book and activities in it support the following Standards and Sample Performance Outcomes for K–2 students:

A physically educated child . . .

Standard 1: Shows skill in movement skills and patterns needed for a variety of physical activities.

1. **Skips, hops, gallops, slides, etc. using proper form.**
   Many of the activities in this book, which incorporate locomotor skills, support this outcome.

2. **Can change directions quickly when traveling forward or sideways in a variety of ways.**
   Several activities in *First Grade Fun, Fitness & Learning* require students to change directions quickly while moving.

3. **Balances on different body parts, like a statue.**
   The "Letter Tag" activity supports this outcome.

Standard 3: Regularly takes part in physical activity.

1. **Participates in moderate to vigorous physical activity on a regular basis.**
   Most of the activities in *First Grade Fun, Fitness & Learning* encourage moderate to vigorous physical activity.

2. **Takes part in a variety of physical activities that include the manipulation of objects (such as tossing a ball) both in and outside physical education class.**
   This book includes several games that involve tossing objects such as balls or beanbags.

Standard 4: Attains and preserves a healthy level of physical fitness.

1. **Participates in a group of locomotor activities (including hopping, walking, jumping, galloping, and running) without getting tired easily.**
   Many of the activities in *First Grade Fun, Fitness & Learning* support this outcome.

2. **Takes part in different games that increase breathing and heart rate.**
   Many of the activities in this book support this outcome.

3. **Knows that physical fitness consists of several different components.**
   The "Fitness at Home" section of this book supports this outcome.

Standard 5: Shows self-respect and respect for others while participating in physical activity.

1. **Follows directions for all-class activities.**
   All the activities in *First Grade Fun, Fitness & Learning* support this outcome.

2. **Uses all equipment and activity space safely.**
   All the activities in this book support this outcome.

3. **Works in a group setting without interfering with others.**
   All the activities in this book support this outcome.

4. **Enjoys exploring movement in tasks done alone.**
   Most of the activities in *First Grade Fun, Fitness & Learning* support this outcome.

············· NCTE/IRA *Standards for the English Language Arts* ·············

This book and activities in it support the following Standards and Sample Performance Outcomes for K–2 students:

Certain activities in this book support one or more of the following standards:

1. **Students read many different types of print and nonprint texts for a variety of purposes.**
   Students must read words, letters, or pictures for many of the activities in *First Grade Fun, Fitness & Learning* .

2. **Students use a variety of strategies to build meaning while reading.**
   Activities in this book focus on many reading skills including vocabulary, phonics, letter and picture identification, grammar, and parts of speech.

3. **Students communicate in spoken, written, and visual form for a variety of purposes and a variety of audiences.**
   While doing the activities in *First Grade Fun, Fitness & Learning,* students communicate verbally, visually, and in writing through movement during games and by drawing, cutting and pasting, and writing on worksheets.

4. **Students incorporate knowledge of language conventions (grammar, spelling, punctuation), media techniques, and genre to create and discuss a variety of print and nonprint texts.**
   The grammar and punctuation activities support this standard.

5. **Students become participating members of a variety of literacy communities.**
   The group language arts activities in *First Grade Fun, Fitness & Learning* help teachers begin to build a literacy community.

NCTM *Principles and Standards for School Mathematics*

Certain activities support the following Number and Operations Standard Expectations for grades Pre-K–2:

1. **Students count and recognize the number of objects in a set.**
   The activities in the "Numbers & Operations" section, among others, support this standard.

2. **Students use various representations to develop understanding of place value and the base-ten number system.**
   The "All Mixed Up!" activity supports this standard.

3. **Students understand the relative position and size of ordinal and cardinal numbers.**
   The activities in the "Numbers & Operations" section support this standard.

4. **Students develop whole number sense and use numbers in flexible ways, including relating, composing, and decomposing them.**
   Activities in the "Numbers & Operations" section support this standard.

5. **Students connect number words to numerals and to the quantities they represent using different physical representations.**
   Activities in the "Numbers & Operations" section support this standard.

6. **Students understand and represent common fractions, such as 1/4 and 1/2.**
   The "Fraction Action" activity supports this standard.

7. **Students understand the meanings of addition and subtraction of whole numbers and how the two operations relate to each other.**
   Activities in the "Numbers & Operations" section support this standard.

8. **Students understand what happens when they add or subtract whole numbers.**
   Activities in the "Numbers & Operations" section support this standard.

9. **Students use a variety of strategies for whole-number computation, focusing on addition and subtraction.**
   Activities in the "Numbers & Operations" section support this standard.

10. **Students use different methods and tools to compute, including concrete objects, mental math, estimation, paper and pencil, and calculators.**
    The "Estimation Station" and other activities in the "Numbers & Operations" section support this standard.

Select activities support the following Algebra Standard Expectations for Grades Pre-K–2:

1. **Students sort, classify, and order objects by a variety of properties.**

The "Sorting Stations" activity supports this standard, as do several activities in the "Fun with Language Arts" and "Fun with Science" sections of the book.

2. **Students recognize, describe, and extend simple sound, shape, or numeric patterns and change patterns from one form to another.**
   The "Predictable Patterns" and "Detecting the Rule" activities support this standard.

3. **Students determine the rules that create repeating and growing patterns.**
   The "Detecting the Rule" activity supports this standard.

Select activities support the following Geometry Standard Expectations for grades Pre-K–2:

1. **Students identify, create, draw, compare, and sort two- and three-dimensional shapes.**
   The "The Shape of Things" activity supports this standard.

2. **Students describe, name, and interpret direction and distance and use ideas about direction and distance.**
   For many of the activities in this book that involve locomotor movements or tossing, students must use ideas about direction and distance.

3. **Students recognize geometric shapes in the world around them.**
   The "The Shape of Things" activity supports this standard.

Select activities support the following Measurement Standard Expectations for grades Pre-K–2:

1. **Students recognize the characteristics of length, volume, weight, area, and time.**
   Activities in the "Measurement" section of the book, along with activities where students time themselves while doing different movements, support this standard.

2. **Students measure using standard and nonstandard units.**
   Activities in the "Measurement" section of the book, along with activities where students time themselves while doing different movements, support this standard.

3. **Students measure by using repeated units of the same size, such as safety pins laid end to end.**
   The "Going to Long Lengths" activity supports this standard.

4. **Students use tools to measure.**
   Activities in the "Measurement" section of the book, along with activities where students time themselves while doing different movements, support this standard.

Certain activities support the following Data Analysis and Probability Standard Expectations for grades Pre-K–2:

1. **Students can ask questions and collect data about themselves and their worlds.**
   The "Fitness at Home" and "Fun with Fitness & Math" activities support this standard.

2. **Students can sort and group objects according to their characteristics and organize information about the objects.**
   The "Sorting Stations" and "Stone Sort" activities support this standard, as do several activities in the "Fun with Language Arts" section of the book.

3. **Students can show data using objects, pictures, and graphs.**
   The "Fun with Fitness & Math" activity supports this standard.

National Science Education Standards

Select activities support the following Physical Science Content Standards for grades K–4:

1. **All students should understand the properties of objects and materials.**
   The "Stone Sort" activity supports this standard.

2. **All students should understand concepts related to the position and motion of objects.**
   Activities throughout this book support this standard.

Certain activities support the following Life Science Content Standards for grades K–4:

1. **All students should understand the characteristics of organisms.**
   Activities in the "Fun with Fitness" and "Fun with Science" section support this standard.

2. **All students should understand the relationship of organisms and environments.**
   The "Blooming Science" activity supports this standard.

Certain activities support the following Earth and Space Science Content Standards for grades K–4:

1. **All students should understand concepts related to changes in earth and sky.**
   The "Weather Workout" activity supports this standard.

This book and selected activities in it support the following Science in Personal and Social Perspectives Content Standards for grades K–4:

1. **All students should develop understanding of personal health.**
   This entire book supports this standard by encouraging movement and physical fitness.

NCSS *National Curriculum Standards for Social Studies*

Activities in this book support the following paraphrased examples for students in the early grades:

People, Places, and Environments: Knowledge

Students understand place, direction, and distance.
The "Go Get It Globe!" and "Movin' with Maps" activities support this standard.

Students use maps, globes, and geographic technology to study the interaction between people and places.
The "Go Get It Globe!" and "Movin' with Maps" activities support this standard.

People, Places, and Environments: Products

Students create a map of their school, community, state, or region that shows they understand location, direction, borders, and physical features.
The "Movin' with Maps" activity supports this standard.

Individuals, Groups, and Institutions: Knowledge

Students understand ideas such as community, culture, role, competition, cooperation, rules, and norms.
The "The Rules Rule!" activity supports this standard.

Power, Authority, and Governance: Knowledge

Students understand that rules and laws create order and protect individuals in a society.
The "The Rules Rule!" activity supports this standard.

Civic Ideals and Practices: Knowledge

Students understand concepts including: dignity, fairness, freedom, common good, rule of law, civics, rights, and responsibilities.
The "The Rules Rule!" and "Patriotic Parade" activities support this standard.

Students understand that participating in a democratic society includes studying issues, planning, decision making, voting, and cooperating.
The "The Rules Rule!" activity supports this standard.

Civic Ideals and Practices: Processes

Students identify and participate in the rights and responsibilities of citizens.
The "The Rules Rule!" activity supports this standard.